EPIDAURUS

CLIO EDITIONS

Art layout: RACHEL MISDRACHE - CAPON

Photographs: N. KONTOS: 37, 40, 41

M. SKIADARESES: 2, 3, 4, 5, 6, 9, 12, 13, 17, 19, 21, 23, 25, 28, 29,

31, 32, 33, 36, 42, 43, 44, 45, 49, 50-71.

S. TSAVDAROGLOU: 1, 7, 14, 22, 24, 30, 35, 38, 39, 46, 47, 48.

ANGELIKI CHARITONIDOU : archaeologist

EPIDAURUS

THE SANCTUARY OF ASCLEPIOS AND THE MUSEUM

2

1. General view of the sanctuary of Asklepios at Epidaurus. In the background, on the left, is the theatre.

2. Statue of the god Asklepios in the National Archaeological Museum (No. 204).

THE SANCTUARY OF ASKLEPIOS AT EPIDAURUS

The Site

The hallowed earth of Epidaurus, where only the ruins of the once magnificent buildings of the Sanctuary of Asklepios now remain, is situated in a densely vegetated plain of the Argolid, surrounded by mountains which embrace it without "suffocating" it. Arachnaio rises up far away to the north. Its summit dominates the entire Argive peninsula to the far off sea. One of the homes of Zeus and Hera was up there. Nearer, to the north of the sanctuary, the gentle slopes of Mt. Titthion fall gradually to the plain. The Epidaurians believed that on this mountain Asklepios was born. Nowadays the locals call it "Theokausto" and "Velanidhia". Opposite, to the south-east, the plain ends and the mountain identified with the ancient Kynortion begins. On one of its slopes the god Apollo has his shrine. Beyond Kynortion, further south, Mt. Koryphaia is distinguishable on the horizon. The goddess Artemis wandered in its woods. On the plain the god Asklepios had his sanctuary.

The Epidaurians were not alone in believing in his healing power. His fame spread throughout the ancient Greek world. Later on it even reached the Romans. A host of believers sought refuge in his Asklepieion (as all sanctuaries of Asklepios in ancient Greece were called) seeking their salvation. And naturally plenty of money was collected in the sanctuary from their offerings. This wealth enabled Art to be expressed in all the glory of the ancient aesthetic and temples and public buildings to be created, wondrous for their decorative and architectural excellence not only in Antiquity but even today.

The ancient Greeks knew how to select for the residences of their gods the most suitable locations in their country. The enchantment the pleasant Plain of Epidaurus proffers the visitor even today was probably one of the reasons why the sanctuary was established there. The climate is mild. The tranquil greenery would, even then, have furnished the sick pilgrims with relaxation and serenity. The sanctuary was also called the Sacred Grove. The plenteous spring waters were another influential factor, though they have no especial pharmaceutical qualities. It was not this which aided the curative powers of the god. It was a blind faith in his philanthropic and miraculous work. The sick who resorted to Asklepios had lost all hope of recovery. They left their homes and took the road to the sanctuary, the blind, the lame, the paralysed, the dumb, the war-wounded, sterile women, all expecting his miracle.

The Ancient City of Epidaurus

The sanctuary belonged to the coastal town of Epidaurus which had been in existence since Homeric times. Homer mentions it with the epithet "ambeloessa" (vine-clad) meaning that its plains were densely planted with vines. Its inhabitants, mostly sailors by occupation, declaimed that their land took its name from the hero Epidauros, son of Apollo. The author Strabo (65 B.C. - 23 A.D.) informs us that the first inhabitants of the region were Kares. When the Dorians came down they lived alongside the Ionians who existed first. The city was built on a small rocky peninsula, the "Island" in the waters of the Saronic Gulf. Systematic excavations have not taken

3. Reconstruction of the sanctuary of Asklepios at Epidaurus, as it was in the period of its acme (A. Defrasse).

place. However, remains of an old rampart are discernible upon the rock. Outside the city, near the harbour, 7 Mycenaean chamber tombs have been found and, in recent years, a small, well-built theatre has been excavated. The present-day adjacent village, Pidaura, as the locals call it, Old Epidaurus officially, was settled in about 1821. A little higher up is a small hamlet bearing the same name. This is Upper Pidaura.

To the north, on the mountain slope about 8 km. from the Saronic Gulf, is a large village officially known as New Epidaurus. The locals call it Piadha. It was in Piadha, in 1822, that the deputies of the nation in revolt met for the 1st National Assembly which declared the independence of Greece and defined its first political act. The inhabitants maintain with pride the old plane tree in whose shadow the notables of the assembly were protected.

Thus all three villages, Old Epidaurus, Upper Epidaurus and New Epidaurus are known by the same name as the ancient city

Excavations

The Greek Archaeological Society (founded in 1837) undertook its first large-scale excavation in the Asklepieion at Epidaurus. It assigned direction of operations to the great archaeologist P. Kavvadhias. Work began in 1881 and by 1928 all the buildings which the visitor to the sanctuary sees today had been discovered. The contribution of the excavation to archaeological scholarship had world-wide repercussions. A new archaeological site was created which contributed much new information to the history of Art. The inscriprions which were found opened up a new chapter of ancient worship and enriched ancient Greek literature. In 1948 the archaeologist I. Papademetriou investigated the shrine of Apollo Maleatas.

The History of the Cult

In most anciet times, when life was still agricultural and towns did not exist, men naturally considered as deities those physical forces and elements allied to their life's

needs. In the region of Epidaurus, much earlier, from Early Mycenaean times (16th century B.C.) the inhabitants worshipped a divinity called Maleatas. In addition to his other attributes he had healing power. His shrine was set up on Mt. Kynortion, higher up than the spring known nowadays as St. Anne's well.

With the formation of towns the manner of thought and way of life changed and a new religion appeared which gradually assumed the form of the Olympian gods. The old faith survived however, as the old divinities were assimilated to the new ones. To this are due the numerous epithets of the gods which are not simply embellishments but have particular cultic significance.

This is also the case with the divinity Maleatas. In the Epidaurus region his cult was replaced by the worship of Apollo and his memory survived as an epithet of Apollo. Along with this he inherited curative power. The worship of Apollo Maleatas continued at the shrine of Maleatas on Mt. Kynortion. In an excavation conducted in 1948 copious remains of sacrifices from the 7th century B.C. offered to the altar of Apollo were revealed. A little to the south the ruins of his Doric temple, built in the 4th century B.C., have survived. Inscriptions carved on the door jambs of a building of the Roman period reveal that the cult of Apollo Maleatas continued there during Roman times.

Nonetheless, the god Asklepios held first place in the religious life of Epidaurus from the 5th century B.C. until the 4th century A.D. When his worship commenced at Epidaurus and when his sanctuary was founded on the site where its ruins still survive has not been elucidated by the excavations nor the written sources either. However, concerning the birth of Asklepios there are many myths.

It seems that in Homer's time Asklepios had not been established as a god for Homer refers to him as a mortal who lived in Thessaly and was a king during the period of the Trojan War. According to Homer, Asklepios had infallible medical knowledge which he taught to his sons, Machaon and Podaleirios. In the Trojan campaign the two sons were commanders of the Thessalian army and doctors at the same time. Indeed, when Menelaos was wounded by enemy arrows it was Machaon who was called upon to treat him.

Subsequent myths refer to Asklepios as a demi-god, born of a mortal woman and the god Apollo which expresses the relation of succession of the divinities in popular belief. Later, Asklepios ascended in the hierarchy from demi-god to god because of the great faith in his miraculous medical knowledge.

Concerning the place of his birth the myths disagree. It would appear, however, that the Thessalian city of Trikke, present-day Trikala, has the most claims. Tradition locates his first sanctuary there. The diffusion of his cult from the north southwards is perhaps associated with the migration of peoples. One myth concerning his birth in Thessaly is related in the epic poem the "Eoies", probably written by the poet Hesiod (circa 8th century B.C.). The same myth with a minor alteration is also to be found in the poet of the "Odes", Pindar (522 - 448 B.C.).

In order to accrue greater glory for their sanctuary, the Epidaurians altered the myth, locating the birth place of Asklepios in their region. The Epidaurian poet, Isyllos (3rd century B.C.) in a hymn dedicated to Asklepios, writes that he was born on Epidaurian soil. The hymn was found written on a plaque and is exhibited in the Museum.

Pausanias (2nd century A.D.) who visited Epidaurus, records the myth related to him by the locals: "When Phlegias went to the Peloponnese to spy out the land he was followed by this daughter Koronis. Her father did not know that she was pregnant to Apollo. When she gave birth she left the boy exposed on Mt. Titthion. A goat suckled him and a dog guarded him. A shepherd passing that way saw the child. There was a divine light all around him. For this reason the shepherd revered him. The child was rescued and followed the divine fate".

All traditions agree that in his youth Asklepios was a pupil of the wisest teacher of his age, the centaur Cheiron who dwelt in Thessaly. Cheiron taught Asklepios medicine and how to distinguish the therapeutic herbs which grew on Pelion. Asklepios showed himself to be superior to his mentor and was recognised by all Greece. His father, Apollo was also a doctor. Another power which he inherited was that of prophecy. Interwoven with the art of prophecy was also the knowledge of death. This is why he was also regarded as a chthonic demon. One of his symbols was the prophetic snake. Just as it emerged silently from the crevices of the earth and was lost again within them, so it knew all its secrets. The snake brought to and interpreted for Asklepios all the hypochthonic mysteries which the earth conceals, death and life. The Epidaurians regarded the snakes in their region as sacred, a demonic force. They were small, blondish in colour and tame. Certainly a vestige of the pre-Hellenic religion.

According to the myths, Asklepios was born through the death of his mother. This is why he knew the secret of death and had the power of resurrecting the dead. However, the abolition of death challenged the natural laws which govern the earth. The great god Zeus, protector of cosmic harmony, would not accept such a change. The mortals did not become immortals. With his thunder-bolt he struck Asklepios dead for wanting to disturb the laws which the great gods had established. The myths give Asklepios this end. Because of his common mortal fate, men felt he was close to them and invoked him to save them from the illnesses which tyrannised their bodies. Many Asklepieia were founded in ancient Greece but all conceded the glory of the god in the Asklepieion of Epidaurus.

The Rituals of the Cult and the Therapeutic Method

The sanctuary of Asklepios, as has been mentioned above, belonged to the city of Epidaurus. The state appointed its highest archon as priest of Asklepios for one year. His responsibilities were both religious and administrative. It was his duty to maintain

6

4. *Relief plaque showing Asklepios seated, a goddess and a winged Nike (National Archaeological Museum, no. 1425).*

5. *Relief showing Asklepios and his family receiving suppliants (National Archaeological Museum, no. 1402).*

6. *Statue of the goddess Hygeia, in the National Archaeological Museum (no. 299) from the sanctuary of Asklepios at Epidaurus.*

the regulations of worship, to protect the votives, the coffers and the management of economic affairs. He was assisted in his work by the Priesthood which consisted of priests, each with specific duties. There were the *Pyrphoros,* the *Nakoros,* the *Naophylakes,* the *Hieromnemones* and others. The canons of worship were traditional and ancient and the sick had to execute them faithfully in order to seek a cure from the god.

When the pilgrims arrived at the Propylaia of the sanctuary they were supposed to know that they were entering a holy place to surrender themselves body and soul to the mercy of the god. An old law forbade women from giving birth within the sanctuary and anyone on the point of death had to be brought outside.

On passing through the Propylaia they saw the preliminary instructions to the believer written up on a stone plaque.

"When you enter the abode of the god
which smells of incense, you must be pure
and thought is pure when you think with piety"

From the Propylaia the pilgrim followed the Sacred Way which led to the temple of Asklepios. Within the magnificent temple stood the statue of the god. Chryselephantine, impressive, with an expression of serenity and benevolence on his face, he listened to the supplications of the faithful. After the temple the pilgrim would halt at the Sacred Fountain. He used the water for the purifications which the regulations called for. Somewhere nearby was the altar. A basic obligation of the pilgrim was to offer a sacrifice "to Apollo and Asklepios" as the tenents explicitly specify. The honouring of Apollo survived but the miracle was attributed to Asklepios. The richest sacrifice was an ox though cockerels were also readily accepted by the god. The poor could make bloodless sacrifices by offering fruits, sweetmeats and other humble things. All those who came from far away were permitted to offer money only. The sacrificed beasts had always to be consumed within the sanctuary.

After the prayers, the purifications and the sacrifices, the ill person had to undergo religious ordeals in order to reinforce his faith and prepare his soul for approaching the god. How and where these holy rites took place is not mentioned anywhere, perhaps because they should remain secret. One opinion is that the Thymele (the Tholos), the circular building located near the temple, was used for this purpose and this is why the mysterious labyrinth is to be found beneath the floor of its cella.

The priests who directed the believers must have created a state of intense auto-suggestion and religious exaltation in them so that the god would appear in their sleep and they would receive his miracle. The compunction was further emphasised by hymns chanted by special singers, the *Paianists.*

After the testing of the soul the moment of "Enkoimesis" arrived. The priests led the invalid to the Abato (or Adyto or Enkoimeterion). This was the building in which he would spend the night of great expectation. Within its hallowed halls, illuminated initially with the subdued mysterious light emitted by the sacred oil-lamps, overcome with religious desire, with an inflamed imagination and anxiety over the outcome, the invalid surrendered his body to sleep. The priests withdrew, leaving the halls in darkness. The god appeared in a dream and performed the miracle. The next morning the sick person awoke cured.

If the supplicant had been cured he should thank the god "offering up to the

7. View of the inside of the museum at Epidaurus in which the finds from the excavations of the sanctuary of Asklepios are exhibited.

doctor" before leaving the sanctuary. Quite often the god himself specified the offering. Other times the priests. The offerings were in accordance with the economic capabilities of the believer. Everything was acceptable. Pottery vases, bronze vessels, 'ex voto' inscriptions, statues, altars, fountains and entire buildings. This is why a host of works of art and buildings embellished the area. The best information about the miracles of Asklepios comes from the tablets (stele), that is the votive inscriptions, where the cured narrate the circumstances of their healing. About 70 written miracles have survived to this day. The ingenuousness of the accounts is impressive:

"A small dumb child came to the sanctuary to beseech the god to give him a voice. After performing all the preliminary sacrifices and rites, the *Pyrphoros,* the servant of the temple, turned to the father of the child and asked him "Do you promise to pay the medical fees within one year if your child is cured?" "I promise" replied the child suddenly".

"Pandharos the Thessalian had blemishes on his forehead. Whilst sleeping in the Abato he had a vision. The god wound a band around his brow. He ordered him to come out of the Abato, to remove the band and dedicate it in the temple. At day-break he arose from his bed and removed the band. His forehead was completely clear. The blemishes were stuck to the band. Then he offered it to the temple."

"A certain woman from Messene, called Nikoboule, longed to have a child. She slept in the Abato and the god appeared in her dream holding a large snake. The snake slept with her. Inside a year the woman gave birth to two sons."

In no written source is the medical intervention of the priests mentioned, throughout the first centuries of the sanctuary's existence. Healing occurred solely with the appearance of the god. With the passing of the centuries, however, the development of medicine began to shake the faith in divine intervention and the sanctuary of Epidaurus, just like the other Asklepieia, was in danger of losing its patrons. For this reason the priesthood was obliged to become modernised. All the conventions of the cult were retained but before the "enkoimesis" the priests asked the invalid to tell them about his ailment and they gave him primary instructions. At night Asklepios appeared once more. However, the sick person now transferred in his dream the advice of the priests, as the counsel of the god. In the morning he related his dream and the priests, using their medical knowledge, interpreted the god's instructions as to the therapeutic method, requesting, of course, that the patient remain within the sanctuary. A characteristic picture of the change is given in a votive plaque dedicated by Apellas in the 2nd century A.D. He suffered from hypochondria and dyspepsia.

"As I was travelling to the sanctuary and approached Aegina, the god appeared and told me not to become very angry. When I reached the sanctuary he instructed me to cover my head because it was raining, to eat bread, cheese, celery, lettuce, to bathe unaided by a servant, to exercise in the gymnasium, to drink lemon juice, to go for walks. Finally the god ordered me to write all this on a stone. I left the sanctuary healthy, thankful to the god."

So the sanctuary not only remained a religious centre but developed into a hospital foundation, even into a social centre with a serene and pleasant environment, hot and cold baths, guest houses, gymnasia, contests and theatrical performances. Because the sanctuary adopted this progressive stance it did not fall into decline but achieved a second acme in the 2nd century A.D. And even when the belief in the Olympian gods was eventually shaken and soul and intellect oscillated in the darkness preceding the triumph of Christianity, Asklepios was the only god who remained until the end close to suffering man. Still in the 4th century A.D. pilgrims went to sleep in the Abato in the hope of a cure.

At the end of the century (395 A.D.) the sanctuary was destroyed by the enemy incursions of the Goths and a few years later (426 A.D.) on the orders of the Emperor Theodosios II the gates of the Propylaia were closed. The fanaticism of the new religion had no respect for ancient art. The destruction was completed by two great earthquakes in the 6th century A.D. which demolished the magnificent buildings, reducing them to the ruins which the excavations have uncovered.

TOUR OF THE SANCTUARY AREA

As has been mentioned above, the date of its founding is not known. The 5th century authors refer to it as being a famous shrine even then. The oldest written finds from the excavation are the marble inscriptions from the 4th century B.C. They are to be found in the Museum and more will be said of them in a special chapter.

The ruins of buildings which have survived on the site commence in the 4th century B.C., the period of its zenith. Usually the visit to the site takes place in the reverse order from that in ancient times. This is because the Museum is visited first and then the visitor sets off for the site. Its entrance, the Propylaia, was exactly on the opposite side, the northern one. The visitor who wishes to understand correctly the operation of the sanctuary must begin his tour at the Propylaia and when he has reached the Guest House he should then visit the Museum. The theatre should be left until last.

Propylaia (1)*

Two wide roads lead to the sanctuary. One starts off from ancient Epidaurus passing between the mountains Titthion and Kynortion. The walking distance was three hours. The other commenced at Argos. Just outside the sanctuary the two roads joined and the visitor soon found himself in front of the magnificent Propylaia. Their role was solely impressive and symbolic for they served no practical purpose since the sanctuary was not enclosed, its extent being delimited only by the mountains. The Gates could not accommodate carriages.

The Propylaia were built in the 4th century B.C. The entire structure stood on a high crepidoma. It was built of porous stone excepting the sima, the roof and the paving stones on the floor which were all of marble. The pilgrim ascended a ramp to the Propylaia instead of a staircase. An identical structure was also to be found on the south side at the exit. Its two façades, north and south, formed Stoas with 6 columns of the Ionic order. Internally, 14 columns of the Corinthian order formed a quadrilateral Stoa. The frieze was embellished with relief bucrania and rosettes. The sima had relief palmette-like decorations and lion-heads. One can see a partial restoration of the Propylaia in the Museum. Before the visitor proceeds to the centre of the sanctuary he sees to right and left ruins of buildings from the time of the Roman Occupation.

Basilica (2)

To the east was a building in the form of a Basilica with 5 aisles and mosaics on the floor. Perhaps it was used as an agora and court-room. With the domination of Christianity a small part of the eastern side of the building was transformed into a church of St. John.

The numbers in parentheses refer to the topographical plan on page 17

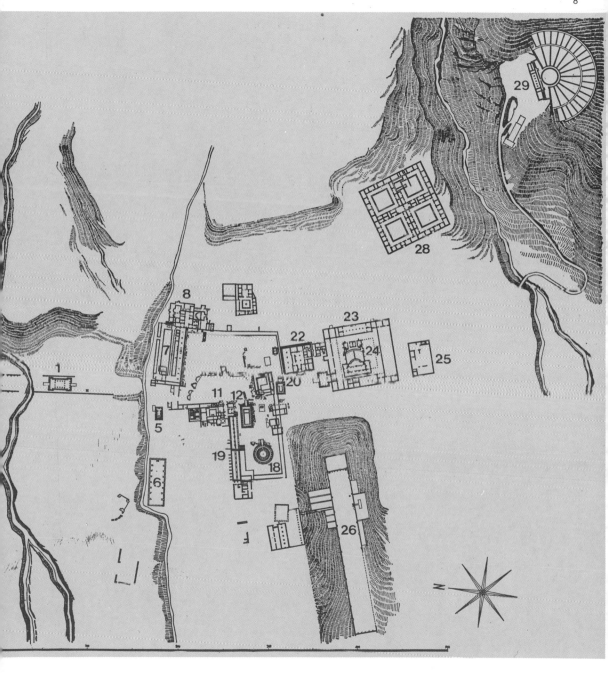

8. Topographical plan of the sanctuary of Asklepios at Epidaurus (after P. Kavvadhias, G. Roux and Ph. Martin).

9. *Plan of the Propylaia of the sanctuary of Asklepios (G. Roux).*

10. *The ruins of the Propylaia of the sanctuary of Asklepios.*

11. *Plan of the basilica at Epidaurus (G. Soteriou).*

12. *The Ionic cornice and part of the columns of the Propylaia of the sanctuary of Asklepios as they have been re-erected in the Museum of Epidaurus.*

9

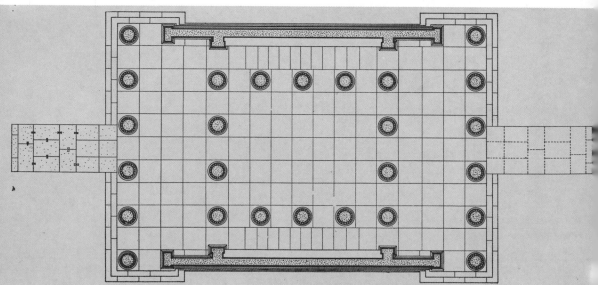

Peristyle Building (3)

To the west are the ruins of a peristyle structure of Roman times with mosaics on the floor. Its purpose is unknown.

Thermes (4)

To the west of number **3** the Thermes are located, also a building of Roman times with an installation for warm baths.

Aphroditeion (5)

Continuing southwards, to the west again, there is a small temple. This has been identified with the temple of Aphrodite and is built of porous stone. It was a prostyle temple with a six-columned stoa. It was built in the 4th century B.C.

Cistern (6)

Further west is a large cistern which was used for the practical needs of the sanctuary.

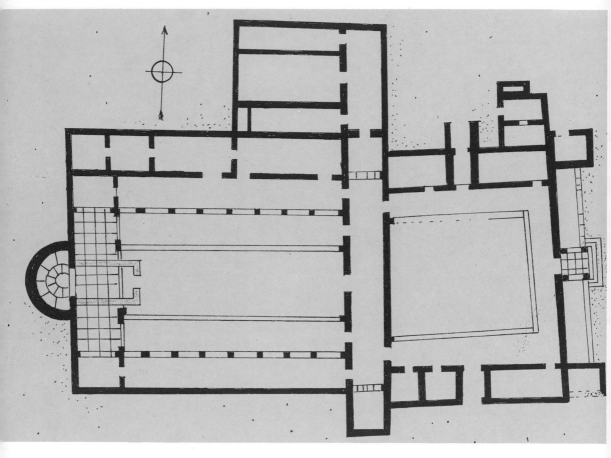

Porticoed Building (7)

On the left, to the east of number **5,** are the ruins of a large building the long south side of which comprises a stoa. Stoas are never absent from ancient cities and sanctuaries for it was there that people congregated for daily contact since they afforded protection from the rain in winter and the strong sun in the summer.

Baths (8)

On the eastern side of the Stoa (number **7**), baths were built in Roman times, "Akoai" as they are named in an inscription found in the excavation. The·name is derived from the Latin word *aqua* which means water. They were luxuriously constructed as the pieces of mosaic indicate and that part of the dado which has

13. *The Roman baths in the sanctuary of Asklepios at Epidaurus.*
14. *The ruins of the temple of Asklepios at Epidaurus.*
15. *Plan of the temple of Asklepios at Epidaurus (G. Roux).*

survived as well as the plumbing installations and circulatory system for hot air which circulated inside the walls. Near here the visitor comes across a fountain and further down, a well.

Residence of Roman times (9)

Temple of Apollo and Asklepios of Egypt (10)

The ruins are attached to number 9. They were built at the expense of the Roman Senator Antoninus in the 2nd century A.D. During the Roman period Egyptian gods were accepted in Greece and frequently identified with the local gods.

In order to continue his tour the visitor must return to the central road of the sanctuary which now narrows between the innumerable pedestals of the "ex votos" with their semi-circular daises and seats, offerings from cured pilgrims.

Bath (11)

Its walls, which are preserved to a considerable height, are built of unworked stones, thus it can be dated, without a doubt, to the Roman period. Perhaps it corresponds to the "Bath of Asklepios" which Pausanius mentions, built by the Roman Senator Antoninus in the 2nd century A.D. Continuing along the Sacred Way, the visitor reaches the heart of the sanctuary, the ruins of the temple of Asklepios.

The Temple of Asklepios (12)

It is considered, on account of its wonderful decoration, to be one of the most notable temples of antiquity. In the partial restoration which has been made inside the Museum of the sanctuary the visitor is able to appreciate something of its grandeur. It took five years to be built from 380-375 B.C. The architect and supervisor of the work was Theodotos.

The temple was peripteros, that is it was surrounded by six columns on its narrow sides and eleven on its long ones, of the Doric order. Its dimensions were 24,50 x 13,20 metres. The building material was porous stone and the surface of the walls was covered with white plaster. The floor was paved with black and white flag-stones. The tiles were of terracotta, the sima, an astonishing example of sculptural art, is of Pentelic marble.

The temple stood elevated above the surrounding area on a crepidoma (all that remains now) and access was via a ramp, rather than steps, built on its narrow eastern side, which led to the peristyle. The internal façade of the temple was embellished with the two columns of the propylon which led to the entrance of the main temple, the cella. The door of the temple, "the great portal", was of wood with ivory decorations attached with golden nails. Thrasymedes, who came from Paros, was the artist. The wooden roof of fir and cypress was also his work. But the most wonderful work of Thrasymedes was the statue of the god which stood at the far end of the cella. Made of ivory and gold, it was larger than life-size, magnificent with an expression of benevolence and wore a long beard. Seated on a throne, he held the *bakteria* in one hand while the other rested on the head of the divine snake. Next to the throne rested reclining, the other symbol of his, the sacred dog. From Pausanias' descriptions it has been confirmed that this statue was depicted on the coins of the city of Epidaurus and in two reliefs discovered in the excavations. The whole of the temple's interior was richly adorned with sculpted and painted decoration. The brilliance of the temple externally was completed by the marvellous statues on the tops of the pediments, the "akroteria" as they are called.

On the pediments were life-size statues of admirable artistry portraying the

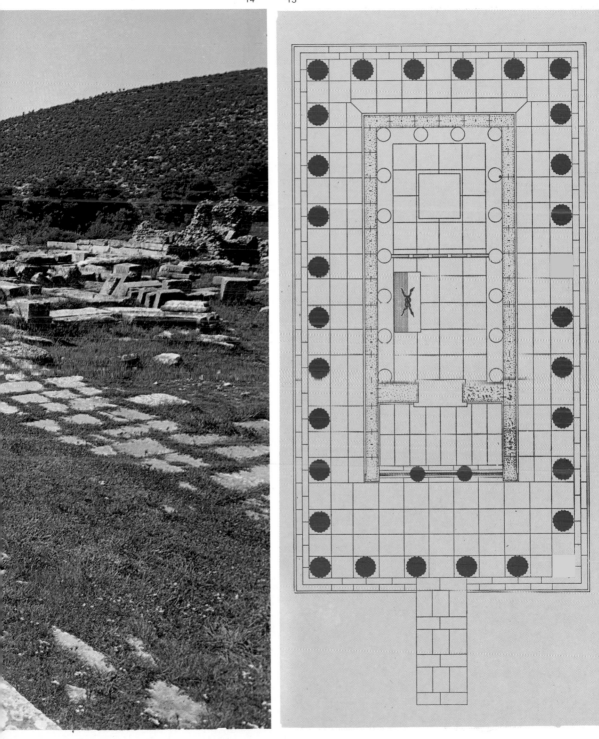

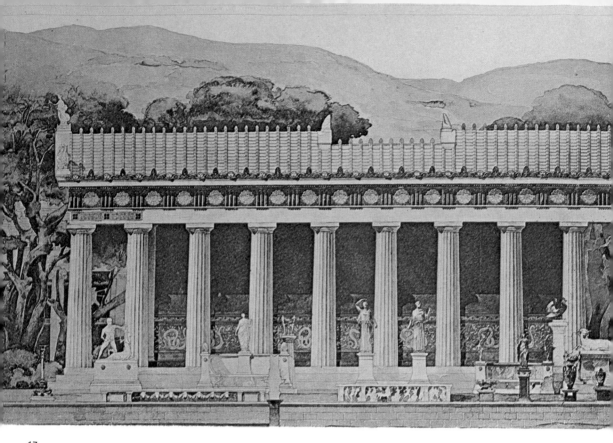

17

16. *Reconstruction of the side face of the temple of Asklepios (A. Defrasse).*

17. *Reconstruction of the façade of the temple of Asklepios (A. Defrasse).*

18. *Section of the temple of Asklepios and view of the cult statue of the god (A. Defrasse).*

19. The ruins of the Tholos, the round building in the sanctuary of Asklepios.

Amazonomachy on the west one and an episode from the Siege of Troy on the east one. Many of the works of art from the temple have been found in the excavations and can be seen in the Museum of the sanctuary and in the National Museum of Athens. Apart from Thrasymedes, two other sculptors are mentioned as having decorated the temple: Hektorides and Timotheos.

The temple of Asklepios, like all the ancient temples, was intended solely to house the statue of the god. The worship of the faithful took place outside the temple, at the altar.

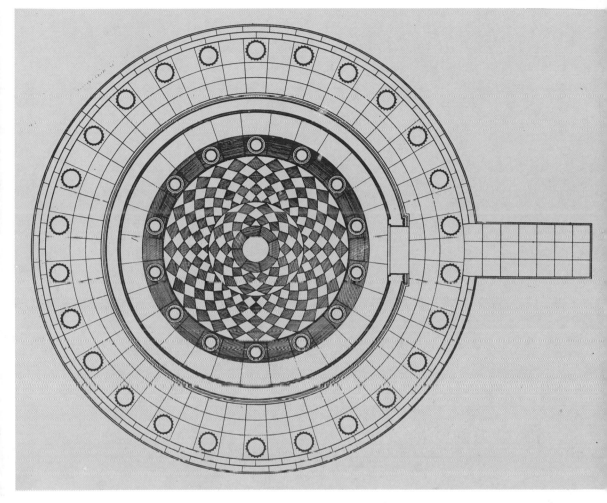

20. Plan of the Tholos in the sanctuary of Asklepios (J. Cami).

Fountain (13)

In front of the temple of Asklepios, after the ramp, a short paved road led to the Sacred Fountain the waters of which were used for purification. Only the base on which a statue stood has survived.

Altars (14,15)

Opposite the temple entrance is a long narrow stone crepidoma perhaps belonging to the newer altar where the sick made sacrifices to the god to help them. To the SE of the temple, in a paved square, was the older altar (no. **15**). Here have been found traces of ashes and remains of sacrifices from the 6th century B.C.

Holy Buildings (16, 17)

Building 16 is dated to the 6th century B.C. and was perhaps the earlier Abato prior to the building of the later one (no. **19**). A small rectangular space in the NW corner perhaps belonged to the earlier temple of Asklepios before his large temple was constructed.

Thymele (Tholos) (18)

West and slightly south of the temple was the most superb, yet the most enigmatic building of the sanctuary. In ancient inscriptions it is called Thymele, Pausanias calls it Tholos. The circular shape of the building is still recognisable even though only three porous-stone circular courses of its foundation have remained. From the myriad bits collected in the excavations, the archaeologist P. Kavvadhias reassembled a section of the Tholos in the Museum and the visitor can form a small picture of this great edifice.

In the area of the ruins of the Tholos, apart from the three circular courses comprising the crepidoma, deep down in the middle are three well-preserved rings

COUPE RESTAURÉE DE LA THOLOS

ORDRE DORIQUE
DE POLYCLÈTE
IVᵉ SIÈCLE
AV. J.C

ORDRE EXTÉRIEU
DE LA THOLOS
D'ÉPIDAURE

ENCEINTE SACRÉE D'ÉPIDAURE

21. *Section and view of the interior of the Tholos in the sanctuary of Asklepios; reconstruction (A. Defrasse).*

22. *Reconstruction of part of the Tholos in the sanctuary of Asklepios (A. Defrasse).*

23. *The external Doric cornice of the Tholos in the sanctuary of Asklepios as it is displayed in the Epidaurus Museum.*

24 - 25. The ruins of the Abaton in the sanctuary of Asklepios.

26. Plan of the Abaton in the sanctuary of Asklepios (P. Kavvadhias).

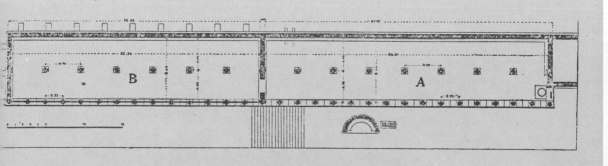

the thickness of which is formed of a monolithic block of porous-stone. These three central stone courses constitute a structure which is perhaps older than the building, probably of the 6th century B.C. The passage from one circle to another is reminiscent of a labyrinth because the low doors opened in the courses for communication between one annular road and another have barriers adjacent to them positioned in such a way that to reach the centre from the outer road, or vice-versa, one is obliged to complete the whole circuit each time. This is why the purpose of the structure is a problem. A host of highly imaginative hypotheses have been advanced. The most likely explanation of the function of the building, based on archaeological data, ancient religion and comparable situations, is that here was believed to be the tomb of Asklepios and this complicated construction was intended to maintain the tomb as a sacred place, far from desecrating eyes. The Tholos kept this crypt beneath the floor of the circular cella. A single round white stone, in the middle of the cella, covered the labyrinth. It was movable and permitted the descent to the underground sacred place.

The Tholos was built in the 4th century B.C., the era of the sanctuary's flourish. Thirty years were required for the completion of this remarkable work of art (360-330 B.C.). Polykleitos was the architect, nephew of the famous Argeian sculptor of the same name. This circular edifice was encircled by 26 Doric columns. The metopes of the cornice were embellished with large relief rosettes. Inside the Doric columns were the walls of the circular cella which stood on an elevated crepidoma. The door (eastern) was of Pentelic marble with relief decoration. The wall of the cella was faced inside and out with black and white marble as well as with relief palmettes, astragals and cymatia. A wonderful painting completed the internal decoration of the wall, by the painter Pausias. Within the cella 14 Corinthian columns formed a concentric circle. The capitals are amongst the loveliest examples of this order. The epistyle and frieze display analogous harmony and plasticity. The floor of the cella on the outside of the Corinthian columns was of white marble paving slabs, the columns stood on black marble and the central area was paved with white and black slabs in the form of a rhombus. The white stone which covered the labyrinth was enclosed by wide black slabs.

All the ceilings of the Tholos were of marble, an achievement of sculpted decoration. The entire roof was also of marble as well as the fully sculpted sima with acanthus flowers and lion-heads.

Abato (19)

The whole of the north side of the temple and the Tholos is closed by a long narrow structure (9,45 × 7 metres), the *Abato* or *Enkoimeterion* or *Adyto,* as an inscription names it, the place in which the patients had to spend the night in order to be cured. All the south side opened into a stoa with a double row of Ionic columns. The eastern section was built in the 4th century B.C. Later, in the 3rd century B.C., a western extension with two storeys was made. A wide staircase connected the new section. At the end of the east stoa there was a deep well. Perhaps the water was considered holy since water played an important part in the purifications of the soul.

Temple of Artemis (20)

South of the old Abato (no. **16**) was the temple of Artemis, the second largest temple in the sanctuary. Artemis certainly had her place beside the god Asklepios. She was the sister of his father, Apollo.

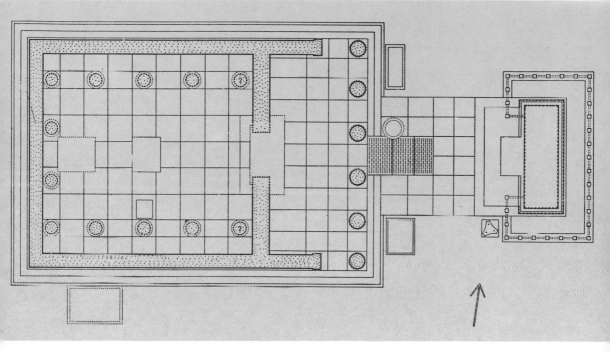

27. Plan of the temple of Artemis in the sanctuary of Asklepios (E. Hansen)

Its dimensions were 13,50 × 9,60 metres. Its façade faced eastwards and six Doric columns marked off its pronaos with one on each side. Twelve Ionic columns traversed the three sides of the interior of the cella. The building material was porous-stone. The sima and tiles were of marble. In the Museum the visitor can see a reconstruction of the NE corner of the temple along with three complete *Nikes,* the acroteria of the pediments.

Epidoteio (21)

The foundations to the NW of the temple of Artemis perhaps belonged to the Epidoteio, shrine of the divinities who belonged to the family of Asklepios. All the members of the family had symbolic names which aided the task of healing: *Hypnos* (Sleep), *Oneiros* (Dream), *Hygeia* (Health) et al. This building, if it actually was the temple of Epidotos, is mentioned in the sources as having been built by the Senator Antoninus in the 2nd century A.D.

To the east of the temple of Artemis was the temple of Themis, the goddess of justice, of the Doric order and almost identical with the temple of Artemis. The cure was justice administered by the gods to their suffering ill worshippers.

All the sacred buildings so far described comprised the centre of the sanctuary. As

28. The ruins of the palaestra or stoa of Kotyos in the sanctuary of Asklepios.

its fame increased, so did its wealth. For this reason magnificent buildings were erected for life's needs.

Palaistra (22)

To the south of the temple of Artemis was the Palaistra, a large building whose use is suggested by its name. The oldest section was the Stoa of Kotyos, perhaps so named after its founder. In the second century A.D. the building was repaired and possibly extended with money from the Senator Antoninus.

Gymnasium (23)

South of the Palaistra extends the gymnasium, a very large building, 75,57 × 69,53 metres. It was used for the preparation of the athletes when, in the latter years of the sanctuary's life, games were organised for the amusement of the ill. Also in the gymnasium those patients whom the god had ordered to take daily physical exercise for the treatment of their body did so under the supervision of special trainers.

One entered the gymnasium through a grandiose Doric, many-columned,

29. The ruins of the gymnasium at Epidaurus.

Propylon which rose up from its north side. The interior of the gymnasium was organised into several appartments, large halls, stoas, baths, out-door areas. It was built at the end of the 4th century B.C. or beginning of the 3rd.

Roman Odeion (24)

In Roman times the Gymnasium was evidently abandoned and left in ruins. Within it, the most recent at the end of the 3rd century A.D., a small Roman odeion was built, that is a small theatre with a skeleton of bricks faced with marble slabs and mosaic on the floor.

Greek Baths (25)

Further south from the Palaistra is the Greek Bath, the *Balaneio,* as the bath-house was called in ancient Greek. It must have been built by the 3rd century B.C. One can see the water conduit in the middle of the east side and the stone bath-tubs inside some of the rooms.

Stadium (26)

The Palaistra, the Gymnasium, the Baths and the Stadium constitute a complete athletic unit. The stadium, which was built in the 4th century B.C. maybe upon an earlier structure to the west of this complex, has been wholly excavated. It is, however, extensively damaged. One may observe interesting points. It was 181,08 metres long and in the shape of a regular parallelogram, that is approximately 1 stadio. Along both long sides there were raised benches of stone, very well-made as the few which have survived indicate.

Along the entire south side of the track the stone water conduit is preserved with basins at intervals for draining the rain water and clearing the course. The conduit ran round three sides of the track. On the north side has survived the underground passage via which the athletes had access to ancillary buildings near the stadium or the athletic area in general. The spectators entered from the narrow south side. On one of the narrow sides the starting point can be distinguished, that is the point where the runners stood before setting off. The place of each runner is marked off by small columns.

The Epidaurian Games, which took place every four years, the Great Asklepieia (founded in 480 B.C. according to Plato) were not among the great Panhellenic games. They had, however, quite a reputation and the poet Pindar (522-448 B.C.) dedicated a few hymns to the victors.

Hippodrome (27)

To the west of the Stadium several *termini* (boundary indicators) attesting the existence of a Hippodrome have been hound.

Hospice or Inn (28)

Outside the sanctuary proper and apart from the Athletic complex was the Inn (the Great Lodge as it is called in the inscriptions) that is the hospice. It is an enormous square building, each side being 76 metres long. Perhaps it was two-storeyed. It was divided into four identical square buildings each having a square courtyard surrounded by stoas and Doric columns. Onto each stoa opened the doors of twenty rooms, therefore it had 160 rooms. The large monolithic thresholds are worthy of attention. In this large hospice the visitors to the sanctuary stayed though not, of course, the sick.

The Theatre (29)

Up until here the visitor has seen most of the important buildings in the sanctuary. Only the visit to the theatre remains. It is considered to be the best-constructed theatre from the whole of antiquity for its elegance, the harmony of its proportions and its acoustics. The visitor should follow the pathway he took initially in order to see the sanctuary, pass in front of the museum and be prepared to admire this great achievement of the 4th century architect Polykleitos. After crossing the *Parodoi* which resemble magnificent Propylaia, he must first halt in the centre of the *Orchestra* (20 metres diameter), as the circular area enclosed by the cavea is called. In the middle was the altar. A whisper is audible even in the uppermost row. The accoustics demand the most difficult technique and especially in the open air.

The visitor must climb up to the topmost row in order to comprehend the perfection

30. *The ruins of the Odeion at Epidaurus, Roman era.*

31. *The ruins of the Greek baths in the sanctuary of Asklepios at Epidaurus.*

32. *The Stadium of Epidaurus, constructed in the 4th century B.C.*

33. *The ruins of the Hospice (katagogion) of the sanctuary of Asklepios at Epidaurus.*

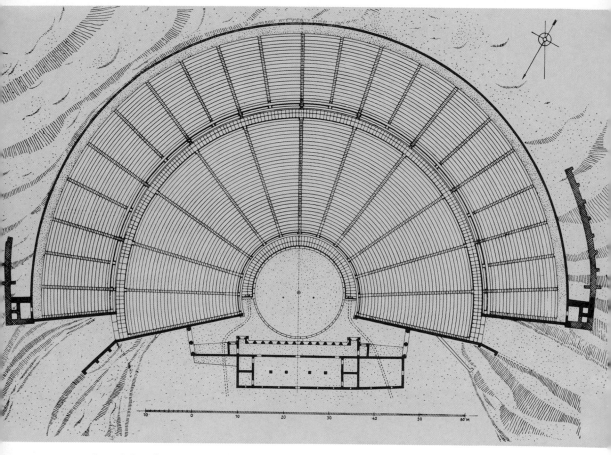

34. *Plan of the Theatre of Epidaurus, built during the 4th century B.C. by the architect Polykleitos.*

of the curve of the cavea. At no point is the spectator prevented from seeing clearly whatever is enacted in the orchestra and on stage. From the upper tiers the magnificent view spreads out and the spectator is confronted with the Epidaurian landscape with its holy edifices without the sun bothering his eyes.

The theatre of Epidaurus never suffered the conversion which other ancient theatres underwent in Roman times. For in these later years, because the type of drama and manner of production changed, the stage was located nearer the audience and the circle of the orchestra was, of necessity, cut. This is why the theatre of Epidaurus constitutes the most splendid example of an ancient theatre. On the façade of the proscenium rested 18 Ionic columns and the surfaces between them were decorated with paintings. At the sides of the proscenium were two projections to which the side scenery was attached. On the proscenium — the *logeio* — the actors played. In the orchestra, the chorus. Behind the logeio arose the *parascenia* (side

35. The Theatre of Epidaurus as seen from afar.

entrances). The cavea (auditorium) was divided into the upper diazoma and the lower diazoma by a paved passage. The lower had 21 tiers of seats and the upper one 34. The spectators entered the lower tiers through two lateral Parodoi and from there went to their seats via radial stairways. They climbed up to the upper rows directly from outside. The specialist scholars maintain that this upper section was an additional extension made at the end of the Hellenistic period in order to increase the seating capacity from 6,200 to 12,300.

During our life-time the theatre of Epidaurus has become known world-wide. Since 1954 the Festival of Epidaurus has been organised each summer when the National theatre of Athens performs ancient tragedies and comedies. A host of people from all over Greece and abroad assembles to watch the productions in a festive atmosphere, while at the same time enjoying the charm of the hallowed countryside of Epidaurus.

36. View of the Theatre of Epidaurus from its stage.

37 - 39. The cavea of the Theatre at Epidaurus.

40 - 42. The gates of the side entrances to the Theatre at Epidaurus, as they are today, after their restoration.

THE MUSEUM

Founded in 1905-1909 by the archaeologist who dug in the sanctuary, P. Kavvadhias, to house the most important finds. Those sculptures which have been taken to the National Museum in Athens have been replaced with their plaster casts. The partial reconstructions of the principal buildings of the sanctuary are exceptionally interesting.

A bust of P. Kavvadhias has been set up in the courtyard. On the outside wall, to the left of the entrance, one of the Ionic columns from the Propylaia has been placed. On the right is a Corinthian column from the Tholos. Also from the Tholos came the sections of the marble sima, with lion heads as water spouts, which are attached to the wall above the entrance.

Vestibule

Here are mainly the inscriptions on large stone surfaces. The majority, excepting the very late ones, are written in the local idiom which belonged to the Doric dialect, the chief characteristic of which is the use of the letter A where the letter H is used in the Attic dialect. In the middle of the gallery stand (to right and left) two large inscriptions. These record the expenditure for the construction of the buildings. That on the right for the Tholos, the one on the left for the temple of Asklepios. They are densely written on both faces and refer in minute detail to the amount of money paid to each contractor and supplier for the work and the material. The bills have been arranged chronologically, the years denoted by the names of the priests of the sanctuary. Frequently the month is mentioned as well. They were written as the work progressed. The amounts are recorded according to a peculiar system, that is with the initials of certain basic numbers, e.g. the letter X means a thousand, E = 100 Π = 5. For the minor amounts, drachmae and obols, vertical lines were used, or horizontal ones or full-stops. These inscriptions are the accounts, the official documents of the city of Epidaurus. The attention and economy with which the works were executed is remarkable.

On the east wall of the vestibule, that is on the one where the entrance is, are the inscriptions of the remedies. These are the best sources of information about the miracles of Asklepios. The first inscriptions on the right side of the door are the earliest (2nd half of the 4th century B.C.). Perhaps they constitute the official record of the cures, compiled by the priests on the opportunity of the construction of the Abato, in remembrance of old glories of the shrine. About 70 of Asklepios' miracles are described. On the left side of the door (facing the wall as always) are inscriptions dedicated by the sick themselves narrating their cure. One of these, from the 3rd century B.C., is in verse, given by the paralysed Ermodikos from Lampsakos. Another one, of Roman times (2nd century A.D.) was dedicated to the god by one Julius Apellas originating from Karia. Towards the SW corner of the vestibule (to the left on entering) to the right of the window, is the most important of the inscriptions (no. 31). It is the Hymn to Apollo and Asklepios, composed by the Epidaurian poet Isyllos. This literary work of art was written in around 280 B.C. and gives important information concerning the cult and history of the sanctuary.

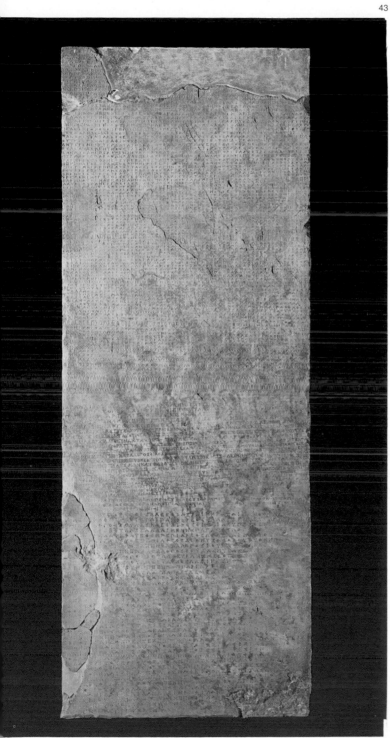

43. The inscription
containing the accounts for
the building of the Tholos
in the sanctuary of
Asklepios.

44. The stele on which are
engraved the "paians"
composed by Isyllos of
Epidaurus and dedicated
to Apollo Maleatas and
Asklepios.

45. The stele relating the
cure of M. Julius Apellas,
in the Epidaurus Museum.

On both sides of the door which leads to the next gallery, on the left stands an inscription containing the Holy Law concerning the sacrifice which the invalid should make to Apollo and Asklepios. It was written in about 400 B.C. in the local dialect. On the right side of the door is the list of the *Thearodokoi,* that is of the representatives of the sanctuary in the various cities with the aim of collecting money for the works. This catalogue is an official document and was compiled between 365-311 B.C. Above the door are shelves on which have been placed terracotta and marble simas. In the small show-case to the left, apart from the other minor objects, are several medical instruments.

Gallery I

Entering the gallery, high up to the left of the door, is the head of an old man, the portrait of a philosopher, perhaps the Stoic Chrysippos, of the Hellenistic period (3rd century B.C.). Also to this period belongs the head to the right of the door as well as the other two on the left (south) wall. On the right wall (above the inscriptions) is a row of statues. A headless statue of a girl (no. 6), which dates from the years 450-425 B.C. is particularly outstanding. The two next ones (nos. 7 & 8) depict Asklepios. They are of the Roman era and imitate earlier prototypes. The two statues before the second window (no. 11 & 12) are of the Hellenistic period and are considered particularly good works of art. After the window (no. 39) is a plaster cast of a statue of Asklepios and no. 40 is of a Nymph. A partial reconstruction of the wall of the Propylaia follows. One can see what the cornice was like with the water-spouts and sima on a building of the Ionic order. After the third window is the plaster cast of a statue of Asklepios as a youth. At the end of the wall is another reconstruction of the internal colonnade of the Propylaia with columns of the Corinthian order. The frieze was embellished with very beautiful reliefs with bucrania and rosettes.

On the opposite side, all along the edge of the gallery, is another reconstruction from the Propylaia. The Ionic columns form a corner of the façade. The height of the columns has been reduced. After the window, on the wall below, is an eccentric monument with triglyphs and metopes which, as certain details indicate, did not belong to a building but to some separate monument, perhaps the covering of an altar. The metopes bear relief representations of the Classical period. On the right metope which is better preserved, Athena gives the helmet to a warrior. It is assumed that this is Asklepios. Perhaps it refers to some martial achievement of the Epidaurians who granted it to the god's help. To the left of the monument, on a plaster plaque, are the most beautiful pieces of sculpture which portrayed a horse-man; perhaps they belonged to the same monument of the Classical period. Before the second window, a plaster cast represents "Aphrodite in Arms".

Between the second and third window, above the large inscriptions and covering the whole height of the wall, have been placed small statues. The majority are plaster copies of originals which are to be found in the National Museum. Beginning from the right on the upper row we distinguish Asklepios with Epione or Hygeia, Roman period, Aphrodite, relatively good art, then perhaps the goddess Artemis. There follow two works of the 4th century B.C., the lower parts of statuettes of Asklepios, Roman period, a statue of the god, of the Roman period, sections of a statuette depicting Aphrodite after her bath, also of the Roman period and others.

Gallery II

R i g h t W a l l. The gallery begins with a partial reconstruction of the sides of the temple of Asklepios. Thus the visitor can see from close to the details of the Doric

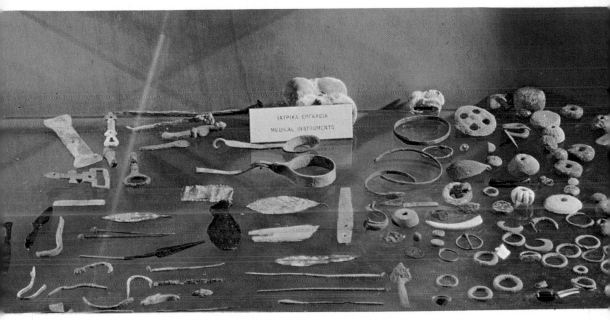

order in a wonderful execution. After the window stands the upper part of a Doric column from the temple. There follows a partial reconstruction of the NE side of the Doric temple of Artemis with triglyphs, metopes and the sima. The sculptures on the sima are impressive, the water-spouts representing the head of a dog and at the extremities, of a boar, not lion-heads as on the other buildings in the sanctuary.

Left Wall. Before the visitor proceeds to the back of the gallery he must return to the beginning, to the left wall, in order to view the reliefs and sculptures which adorned the temple of Asklepios and of Artemis. Even though they are copies (the originals are in the National Museum) their beauty is evident. The sculptures from the pediments of the temple of Asklepios have been put on shelves. They are life-size statues of exceptional artistic merit. From the Amazonomachy a mounted Amazon is particularly noteworthy, as she charges to strike her opponent. In her attacking gallop — the movement of the horse is also remarkable — the wind presses the chiton against her body and all the skill of the artist in moulding the female body is visible as also in the billowing pleats of the chiton. The fallen warrior is also a lovely piece.

Higher up is the Acroterium from the west pediment of the temple. Life-size marble statues surmounted the three corners of the roof which the pediments formed. They literally appear to fly into the heavens. At the top stood, or rather flew, the statue of Nike. Her chiton is blown aside by the wind in copious folds while leaving her richly curved body marked out. In her right hand, according to the specialists, she held a partridge, the symbol of healing. At the corners of the pediment flew the *Aures* (Breezes) on horses with elegant bodies and richly pleated chitons.

On the wall between the second and third window are the casts of the two reliefs of Asklepios seated on a throne. (The marble originals in the National Museum are numbered 173 and 174). They perhaps copy the chriselephantine statue in the temple. They are considered good works; circa 400 B.C. Further right, high on the wall on shelves, are the acroteria from the temple of Artemis. They are three charming female statues of Pentelic marble with lively movement which represent Nikes, without wings by now.

All the rest of the gallery is taken up by a partial reconstruction of the Tholos. The height of the gallery is not sufficient for this splendid edifice and it has been reduced. The visitor can, however, study the decorative wealth of the architectural members. From these the aesthetic spirit which characterised the 4th century B.C. is apparent. On the left, the external colonnade has been reconstructed, the peristyle. Upon the Doric column rests the epistyle with triglyphs and metopes. In each metope a large relief rosette. The epistyle is crowned by the sima with relief lion-heads, palmettes and acrocerama. Through the column the wall of the circular cella is visible. The roof of the peristyle has not been attached in the correct position but a section of it has been placed upright on the opposite wall, on the right of the gallery. Nevertheless, the visitor can admire the very beautiful relief flowers in the square panels. Beside the wall stands the richly sculpted marble door which opened into the inner area of the Tholos, the cella.

Behind the Doric epistyle and wall is the reconstruction of the internal colonnade of the Tholos with the Corinthian capitals and ceiling. The flowers in the panels are different from those of the ceiling outside. They are very sappy and full of natural flexibility. Continuing, a sample of the internal floor is laid out with white and black marble slabs in the form of a rhombus. On shelves on the walls are sculpted marble decorations coming from a large acanthus which must have adorned the top of the conical roof of the Tholos.

The Corinthian column on the left was found, kept safe since ancient times, in the earth. The scholars think it may be the model made by Polykleitos as an example for the craftsmen working on the Tholos and afterwards it was guarded as a votive to the god. The rest of the gallery is filled by a reconstruction again of the external colonnade of the Tholos. It is a section of the Doric epistyle with triglyphs and rhomboids in the metopes. The sima has beautifully carved reliefs of natural motifs, lion-heads and acrocerama.

49

46 - 48. Minor objects,
items of every-day use and
medical instruments,
found during the
excavation of the sanctuary
of Asklepios at Epidaurus.

49. Marble statue
portraying Asklepios as a
young man (National
Archaeological Museum,
no. 1809).

51

162

50. Marble statue of the goddess Hygeia, in the Epidaurus Museum.

51. Headless body of a winged Nike coming from the temple of Asklepios (National Archaeological Museum, no. 162).

52

52. *Equestrian statue of an Amazon, coming from the pediment of the temple of Asklepios at Epidaurus (National Archaeological Museum, no. 136).*

53. *Marble statue of the goddess Athena, in the Epidaurus Museum.*

54 - 55. Statues portraying
Nereides or Aures which
were utilised as acroteria
on the temple of Asklepios
(National Archaeological
Museum, no. 156 - 157).

56. Statue of Nike,
possibly the central
acroterium of the temple of
Asklepios at Epidaurus
(National Archaeological
Museum, no. 155).

57 - 58. Reliefs with a
representation of the god
Asklepios seated (National
Archaeological Museum,
no. 173 - 174).

59 - 61. Marble statues of Nikes, coming from the temple of Artemis at Epidaurus (National Archaeological Museum, no. 159 - 161).

62. Part of the cornice of the temple of Asklepios as it is displayed in the Epidaurus Museum.

63. Corinthian capital considered to be the "model" for identical capitals in the Tholos of the sanctuary of Asklepios.

62

63

64

64. *Part of the cornice of the temple of Artemis as it is exhibited in the Epidaurus Museum.*

65-66. The Tholos of the sanctuary of Asklepios. Section of the roof of the cella as it is displayed in the Epidaurus Museum.

65

67. *The Tholos of the sanctuary of*
Asklepios. Section of the roof of the
peristyle in the Epidaurus Museum.

68. *Detail of the roof of the peristyle of the*
Tholos of the sanctuary of Asklepios in the
Epidaurus Museum.

69 - 70. *Restoration of part of the Tholos of*
the sanctuary of Asklepios in the Epidaurus
Museum.

71. *Internal Corinthian column from the*
Tholos of the sanctuary of Asklepios with the
cornice, Epidaurus Museum.